Book Love

{ Help Your Child Grow from Reluctant to Enthusiastic Reader }

D0873546

melissa taylor

CHILDREN'S DEPARTMENT
Falmouth Public Library
300 Main Street
Falmouth, MA 02540

creator of

Imagination SOUP

© 2012 by Melissa Taylor

All rights reserved. No part of this book may be reproduced in any form without permission in writing from the author, except in the case of brief quotations embodied in critical articles or reviews.

Edited by: **Toni Sciarra Poynter**

Cover Design: **Georgia Morrissey**

Interior Design: **Idea Stylist, Lisa Valuyskaya**

Author Photo: **Tasha Christensen**

ISBN-10: 0988412411

ISBN-13: 978-0-9884124-1-5

Par /Teach
I
372.4
Tay
Mari

CHILDREN'S DEPARTMENT
Falmouth Public Library
300 Main Street
Falmouth, MA 02540

Disclosure of Material Connection: Some of the links in this book are "affiliate links." This means if you click on the link and purchase the item, I will receive an affiliate commission. Regardless, I only recommend products or services I use personally and believe will add value to your life. I am disclosing this in accordance with the Federal Trade Commission's 16 CFR, Part 255: "Guides Concerning the Use of Endorsements and Testimonials in Advertising."

To Jeff,

Thank you for always believing in me.

Table of Contents

Chapter Three: **Too Blurry**   **41**

Chapter Four: **Too Tricky**   **49**

Introduction

I remember when my now ten-year-old didn't like books. And when my now seven-year-old didn't want to read. She'd happily listen to a story, but reading on her own? Not so much.

Guess what my favorite activity is? Reading. And I'm an elementary school teacher.

How could my kids not like reading?

I'd take that challenge.

You will too, right? You bought this book!

Each of my kids disliked reading for different reasons. And that's what makes this book different from other books about motivating readers: it's not a one-size-fits-all approach. Different kids have different (and often multiple) reasons for being reluctant to read. I'll help you figure out why your child doesn't love to read share lots of ideas for what to do about it.

Kids are beautiful, ever-changing puzzles.

Some kids are easy to figure out. They hand us their puzzle pieces and help us put them together. Others, like our reluctant readers, aren't so easy. We must discover their unique puzzle— and help them discover it, too.

This book will help you do that for the unique and beautiful puzzle that is your child. It will encourage you to think, search, and try out different ideas. As you do, you'll come ever closer to finding the right combination of ways to help your child develop a better relationship with books and reading. By the end of this book, you and your child will know each other better—and you'll have the joy of watching him go from hating reading to loving it.

And guess what? No teaching certificate required!

Also, visit the *Book Love* website at Book-Love.net for links to all articles, products, and resources mentioned in *Book Love.*

Here's my hand to hold. **I know you can do this.**

So, let's get your reluctant reader reading!

Chapter One: **Why?**

Why don't kids like to read?

There are all sorts of reasons, in all sorts of combinations. But they boil down to certain key underlying issues we'll start to explore here. In order to help your child love to read you need to know the underlying issue for why she doesn't like to read.

In my experience, kids dislike reading for four general reasons, which we'll explore in the next several chapters:

1. Too boring

2. **Too blurry**

3. **Too tricky**

4. **Too "sitty"**

Too Boring

Too boring means one of two things: either the reading level is too hard, or your child hasn't found the right book or subject that gets him hooked. I'll help you figure out which issue applies and give you action steps for what to do about it.

Too Blurry

Vision, learning difficulties, and the ability (or inability) to pay attention all powerfully affect learning. How do you know if one of these is a problem for your child? We'll look at the red flags and what to do next.

Too Tricky

Particularly if you love reading and never had any problems learning to read, it's easy to forget that reading is one of the hardest things your child will learn to do. I'll help you determine the problem and what you can do to help.

Too "Sitty"

Sitting still doesn't appeal to many kids, mine included. If you have a child who doesn't like to sit and read, I'll help you find alternatives to sitting—all of which include reading!

Plan for Success

Here are some essential guidelines for setting your child up for success as you help him learn to love reading.

Remember:

Reading doesn't happen because your child turns six. Just because schools are pushing your child to read in kindergarten does not mean that your child, your individual little person, is ready to read. In fact, he probably isn't.

Don't push him. Please.

Reading will happen—when your child's brain is ready. The exception? When there is a learning disability. You'll start to suspect a learning disability when you notice the red flags listed in Chapter Three, symptoms such as poor memory, low comprehension, and confusion with directions. Otherwise, don't worry. If you push, you'll almost guarantee that he'll think reading is awful, too hard, a punishment, a torture . . . you get the idea. Sure, he may figure out reading eventually, but will he love it? No.

Read Aloud Daily
(Even If Your Child Can Read Silently)

Want to know the biggest predictor of your child's reading success?

You. **Reading to him. Every day.**[1]

Read aloud to your child every day, from birth to tween. Or until he asks you to stop. Keep going as long as you can. Why? Because you'll build vocabulary, expand background knowledge, and talk about new and difficult concepts. Not only that, it's a time to relax and bond with your child.

Even if all you can commit to is five minutes a night. Do that. And feel free to be dramatic when you read. Especially with younger children, make voices, make faces, act it out. Make it fun!

Limit the Biggest Distraction

Turn off the TV as much as possible. That goes for you as well as for your child.

Maybe you'll curse me now, but when your child chooses to curl up with a good book instead of being hypnotized by the TV, you'll thank me. Get used to no TV except on the weekends. You can't expect a child to focus on reading with the TV distracting him.

Try it for two weeks and see what happens.

Engage in Grown-Up Reading

The apple doesn't fall far from the tree, right? Kids copy what we do.

Here's your chance to read that book you've been wanting to read. So, read a book. Or two. Or ten. Show your child how you choose your books. Talk about the ones you want to read. Demonstrate how you make time for reading, even a little bit, every day.

Show him how readers behave by showing that **you're a reader.**

Keep Picture Books in the Picture

Picture books are valuable reading! As your child gets older, don't forget about them in favor of chapter books. After all, don't you sometimes enjoy an easier read alongside more challenging ones? Our kids are no different. Let them have their picture books. In many cases, however, the reading level of picture books is much higher than you'd think—up to fifth grade in some cases.

Offer Choices

Remember being told what to read in school? It's not motivating.

Kids get enough of that in school, so let them choose their own books to read. You can offer ideas and choices; you can guide their selection; you can even teach them how to determine whether a book is at their reading level . . . *but let your child make the final choice(s).*

Go to Book-Love.net to download the "Rights of the Reader" from Walker Books and Daniel Pennac, and use it to guide your reading lives.

Help Your Child Make the Time

It seems like a no-brainer that kids need time to read, but often their schedules are so jam-packed that they don't have the time and mental space needed for reading. Look at your family schedule. Is there time for each child to sit down and read for 10 to 30 minutes every day—and for you to read together for at least some of that time?

Move things around in your schedule if there isn't.

If no one in the family is making time for reading, your child will wonder: How important can it be?

Reading is important. Make time for it.

Chapter Two: Too Boring

Ask your child, "Why don't you like reading?"

An "it's too boring" answer means this chapter is for you.

First, show empathy. "I know what you mean. Sometimes books are boring."

Then ask more questions. You need more information.

You want to find out what boring means.

Ask questions such as:

"Do you remember any books that weren't too boring?"

"Have you ever liked a story that wasn't boring?"

"When you read, do you think all books are boring?"

"If you could write a not-boring book, what would it be about?"

"Does boring mean too hard?"

"Does boring mean you don't really like what it's about?"

Don't worry if your child doesn't answer your questions. Keep these questions in mind— and your goal of helping him enjoy reading in mind—and ask when it's a better time.

If Boring Means Too Hard

Boring can be kid-code for other issues a child can't articulate. If boring is code for too hard, you'll find ideas for her in Chapter Four.

If Boring Means Boring

If boring really means boring, that's actually good news, because it's a pretty fixable problem. We just need to find your child a book she likes, er, loves.

One of the best ways to get your child to love books is to find the subjects and stories your child *loves.*

Obsessions

Obsessions. That's kid-speak for kids' interests. What are your child's obsessions? Fill them in below (or add categories):

Toys ....

Games ....

Animals ....

Foods ....

Friends ....

TV shows ....

Movies ....

Careers ....

Sports ....

Colors ....

....
[Fill in]

....
[Fill in]

....
[Fill in]

Knowing your child's obsessions will lead you to the books your child **wants to read.**

(She just doesn't know it yet. That's why you'll ease her into them.)

Nonfiction books are easiest to match with your child's obsession—be it firefighters or building with LEGOs.

Choosing fiction aligned with your child's obsessions is a bit more challenging, but it's not impossible.

To get you started, use the book lists in Chapter Twelve categorized by obsession.

Break the Bedtime Rules

This is a great way to get kids reading. Since almost no kid wants to go to sleep right away, give your child the choice between going to bed or staying up late to read a book.

Breaking the rules might just motivate your child to read.

Oh, and skip buying a reading lamp. Buy a headlamp—the light is brighter and covers a wider area. Then kids can also read in the car at night (including during longer trips where it's tempting to let them overdose on video games or movies), in a tent or in a cabin at camp, or when staying over with friends or relatives.

Get Silly

Most kids are silly. Get books that will crack your kids up—no matter their age, gender, or interest. When in doubt, go for potty humor, especially with boys. If that doesn't work, try joke books. You'll find a list of funny books in **Chapter Twelve**.

Get Social: Book Clubs

Starting a mother-daughter book club encouraged my reluctant reader. We formed the club about midway through her year in first grade. She and I took turns reading chapters to each other, which was lovely bonding time. We read one or two chapters a day, which made it manageable to finish the book within the allotted time. The reward of seeing friends, playing, eating snacks, and having a little chat about the book was extremely motivating—and why I recommend book clubs for reluctant readers.

Start a parent-child book club of your own. Gender- and grade-specific book clubs usually work best because of more common reading levels and interests.

1. Invite between six and twelve friends to be in the group. Choose them together with your child. You could even make and send the invitations together.

2. Rotate houses. The host gets to select the book.

3. Consider the ages of the children and pick a book that is generally appropriate for that age group. (Ask a librarian or your child's teacher to advise you on book choice—then let your child pick from the choices.)

4. Provide snacks, drinks, and prepare three to four discussion questions.

5. For more book club ideas, visit "It's Not Too Late to Start a Summer Book Club."
http://imaginationsoup.net/2012/08/its-not-too-late-to-start-a-summer-book-club/

Geek Out

Kids love technology. Use that love to develop a love for reading, too.

There are good electronic books (e-books) that kids can read on Kindle, Nook, iPad, a laptop or desktop computer, or even on a mobile device like an iPod Touch.

Kindle:

This is Amazon.com's hand-held book reader, featuring a screen that seems like a book page. Kindles are available in a variety of prices and sizes with different features, including Wi-Fi. Kindles are best for chapter book readers, since they don't offer a picture book selection.

Nook:

The Barnes and Noble hand-held readers are available in black and white and color with features like GlowLight for night reading and Wi-Fi. The Color Nook offers a wide variety of picture books and chapter books for young readers.

iPad:

The iPad offers the most reading options for all ages of readers. Browse for book apps in the app store, search in iBook, a free app linked to Apple's eBookStore, or download the iPad Kindle app linked to Amazon's bookstore for use on the iPad. My favorite books for iPad are in Chapter Twelve.

Smartphones:

Many book apps are available for cell phones—iPhones and Androids in particular. Tiny print alert: I don't care for reading on a small screen even if I can enlarge the type size but I am old; maybe your kids won't mind.

Computer:

Your home computer can access websites or programs on CD offering reading practice and books. Library cardholders can borrow e-books from their public library for FREE! Isn't that amazing? (http://www.overdrive.com/resources/drc/)

Comics and Graphic Novels

Comics and graphic novels (full-length comic-style stories) don't deserve the lack of status they've traditionally been given as resources for reading. Both are stories told in a visual format and very much count as reading.

I think you should encourage your kids to try comics.

For 8 reasons why your kids should read comics, visit this article on Imagination Soup: http://bit.ly/Rvikf0.

Book Bucks

Give your child money to spend on books—either at the bookstore or at a yard sale. With young children, instead of money, give them a "book buck" worth one book of their choosing.

Consider rewarding your kids with bookstore dollars for accomplishing reading goals.

Win-win, right?

Library Card

Get your child her own library card.

Then, let her use it. Don't limit the number of books she borrows—at least, not too much. Maybe even let her attempt to max out her card, just for fun—and see if she can read every book she checked out.

Trust me on this. It works.

Book Storage

Give your child spaces to store his books. Buy bookshelves for lots of locations in the house. When I say bookshelves, I mean anything that can hold books. Get creative: baskets, boxes, pails, tubs, crates, cubbies, wagons, book slings, et cetera. Encourage your child to come up with ideas for special places to store his books so he can get them whenever he wants.

Book Nook

Make an enticing place for your child to curl up with a good book. Look at your spaces and use your imagination. With your child's help, designate a tent, corner, or closet for his reading nook.

Add some:

- pillows
- blankets
- curtains
- books
- decorations—quotes, signs, posters of books, kid-made artwork

- hanging swing
- comfy chair (**How about a beanbag chair?**)
- rug or carpet squares
- sleeping bag
- lamp

See what reading magic happens in this new, cozy, just-for-your-child space.

Read Books with Movies

Want to see the movie? Read the book first. Or vice-versa. Then have fun comparing them. What was in the book that wasn't in the movie? Did the movie match the way your child imagined things? Which one did your child like better, and why? (In my humble opinion, usually the book beats the movie hands-down.) Find a list of books with movies in Chapter Twelve.

Encourage Your Child to Read to a . . .

doll, dog or cat, stuffed animal, little brother or sister, grandparent, Skype relative, . . .

Start the Book; Let the Child Finish

I do this all the time. I'll start reading a book I think my daughter will like. My goal is to her hooked on the story. Then, I suddenly get "busy" so that we stop reading it.

Often, not too long after, she just cannot resist that book—she has to see what happens.

Diabolical? Oh, yeah. (And it totally works!)

Lift, Pull, Turn

You know those books that make you do something: Lift the flap, pull the tab, and turn the wheel? There are lots of those books and they're tons of fun—and not just for preschoolers.

Read Magazines

My kids sometimes love magazines, sometimes not. Let your child browse magazines at the library and see what she likes before you commit to buying a subscription. See Chapter Twelve for magazine recommendations.

Get Hooked on a Series

See if you can find a book your child loves that is part of a series. Then you'll have more to read that continues the adventures of the characters, or on related topics. Sometimes you can find a series that's based on your child's obsession and extend her interests (and reading) from there. A child who loves dinosaurs might read books in a series that includes dinosaurs and then moves into other topics on prehistory or archeology.

Read a Banned Book

For some reluctant readers, reading a banned book dangles irresistible forbidden fruit. I have a selfish reason for doing this with my kids: I usually love all the banned books. They make me think. See my favorite banned books in Chapter Twelve.

Read with a Bookmark or Pointer

One of my kids loves to use a bookmark to read. She marks the line she's reading by holding the bookmark just under the line. For her, bookmarks are gold—she collects them from the library, from bookstores, and often makes them herself.

But my other child likes to use a reading pointer when we read together. She uses the pointer to track the words. Give it a try. See what your child prefers.

Read the Captions

One Imagination Soup reader lets her son watch SpongeBob SquarePants without sound. It's the only way she'll let him watch cartoons because she makes it educational—he reads the captions. Would this work for your child, too?

Product Recommendations
(To Make Reading Not Boring)

Headlamp

Pointers

Finger Pointer

Monster Finger Pointer

Student Pointers Set of 8

Bookmarks

Harry Potter Wand and Bookmark Set

Magnetic I-Clips: Live Love Laugh

Wizards and Dragons

Chapter Three: Too Blurry

Sometimes children say that reading is boring when in fact some other difficulty is causing the problem.

If you've tried making reading interesting for your child, but he's still resisting reading, there might be other issues that are making reading hard for him.

If your child has an underlying medical problem interfering with reading, of course he'll hate to read.

What are the warning signs that warrant further evaluation?

Is There a Vision Issue?

A friend recently told me how fidgety and impatient she gets when she tries reading without her glasses for even a few minutes. Is your child's reluctance to read coming from issues with sight or vision?

Note that I made a distinction just now between sight and vision. **That's because vision is a brain activity; sight is the eye's work.**

You might also be surprised to learn (I was) that academic success requires 17 different visual skills, and seeing 20/20 is just one of them.

Dr. Jina Schaff, O.D. explains,

"When we read, we have three motor movements before we can process what we are reading. We have to 1) converge: aim our eyes at the target, 2) focus: make the print on the page clear, and then 3) track along the page. If any of those motor movements are deficient, you will work twice as hard to read. If your brain is focused on the motor movements, there is little left for comprehension. This will affect the child's performance in school."

Vision Red Flags

Signs of a possible vision problem in your child include:

- squinting
- eye rubbing
- burning, itching, watery eyes
- headaches
- trouble reading words he already knows
- losing place while reading
- saying that the words look blurry
- bumping into things

A vision screening is not enough to pick up most issues. If you suspect your child has a vision issue —such as dyslexia, double vision, focusing problems, visual processing problems, or poor visual memory—you'll need to schedule her for a comprehensive exam (not a screening) with a qualified developmental optometrist.

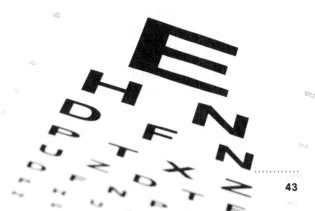

Is There a Learning Issue?

Jane Healy, Ph.D. writes that "learning differences, which are the cause of many school and personal problems, are variations in the way the brain processes information."[2]

I want to emphasize this point because it's important to remember that

- learning differences don't measure or reflect intelligence

- learning differences often co-exist with giftedness

So, if you're feeling hesitant about having your child assessed for learning differences, remember that a learning difficulty is *not* lack of intelligence. Don't wait. If you suspect a learning problem, the sooner you figure it out, the better things will be for your child. Denial just prolongs your child's discomfort and stress. I've seen too many parents try the "denial will make it go away/he'll grow out of it" route. It doesn't work, as you can imagine.

Learning Disability (LD) Red Flags

According to the National Center for Learning Disabilities, signs of LD are:

- spelling the same word differently in a single document
- reluctant reading or writing
- trouble answering open-ended questions
- weak memory skills
- slow work pace
- frequent misreading of information
- easily confused by instructions
- poor organizational skills

I'm not an expert. These are only some issues that you would see repeatedly in children who face learning difficulties. If you are concerned, ask your pediatrician for his or her recommendation on the next step.

You are legally entitled to request an evaluation of your child under the Individuals with Disabilities Education Act (IDEA). You can learn more about IDEA and the evaluation process at the National Center for Learning Disabilities website (www.ncld.org).

Is There an Attention Issue?

Attention Deficit Hyperactivity Disorder (ADHD) is a problem with inattentiveness, impulsivity, and in some cases, over-activity. Nearly one in ten school-age children are diagnosed with ADHD, according to the Centers for Disease Control and Prevention (CDC) (http://www.cdc.gov/).

Signs of ADHD

According to the National Center for Learning Disabilities, signs of ADHD are:

- difficulty paying attention
- daydreams a lot
- doesn't seem to listen
- is easily distracted
- forgets things

- frequently squirms or fidgets
- talks too much
- acts and speaks without thinking
- interrupts others

Because ADHD affects learning significantly, once again don't wait to have your child assessed. A diagnosis doesn't automatically mean you'll have to put your child on medication. It does mean you'll have more information about how your child's brain works, and from there you can explore options and make a more informed decision about the best way to help your child. That's what's most important.

For more information, visit:

National Resource Center on ADHD (www.help4adhd.org)

Children and Adults with Attention-Deficit/Hyperactivity Disorder (www.chadd.org)

Other Issues that Interfere with Learning

In my experience as both teacher and parent, other issues beyond LD can interfere with a child's ability to learn including:

Anxiety, Depression, and Stress

Brain researcher, David Sousa writes, "children must feel physically safe and emotionally secure before they can focus on the curriculum." Emotions either support or inhibit learning.[3]

Lack of Sleep

Children need nine hours of sleep a night for memory storage.[4] If your child isn't getting adequate sleep, it will affect her ability to learn.

Sensory Processing Disorder

Sensory Processing Disorder (SPD) disrupts a child's ability to function in everyday life. These children's bodies can't organize the sensory signals (touch, sight, hearing, taste, smell) causing interference in daily activities and routines.[5]

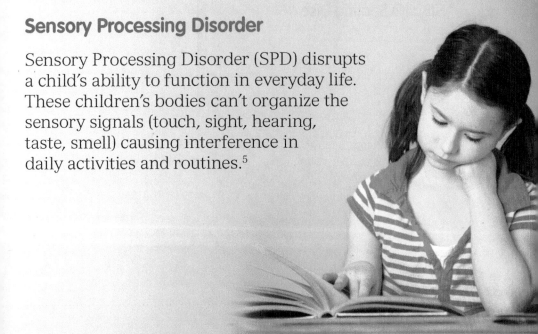

Product Recommendations
(To Make Reading Not Blurry)

Colored Overlays

Reading Trackers

Reading Guide Strips

FitBall® Seating Disc

Chapter Four: Too Tricky

Reading is hard. No doubt. But most kids won't tell you that it's hard. Instead they'll say, "It's boring" or "I don't like it." The process of learning to read is complex, and there are numerous approaches to teaching reading, too. At any point along the way, there can be breakdowns in the child's understanding.

Dig a little deeper and see if you can find where they're feeling overwhelmed and confused.

Digging Deeper

Starter Questions

"When you read, can you figure out the words, or is that kind of hard for you?"

"When you read, does it seem confusing to you?

"What about reading is the hardest thing, do you think?"

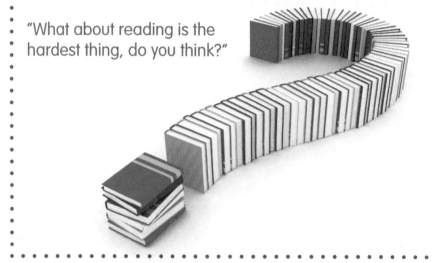

Quick Phonics Assessments and Activities

This is a choose-your-own ending section. Below you'll find a series of simple home assessments to help you identify trouble areas your child may be having. Follow along until you encounter a question to which your answer is "no". At that point, stop and do the suggested activities for that skill. When you think your child has improved enough with the skill, continue on with these assessments where you left off.

Letter Sounds Assessment

1.   Show your child an index card with the word: CAT

2.   Ask your child: "Can you tell me the sounds in this word?"

3.   Then ask: "What word is it?"

If your child knows, go to the next assessment.

If not, work on the Alphabet Activities in Chapter Six and the Phonics Activities in Chapter Eight.

Rhyming Assessment

1.   Ask your child: "What are some words that rhyme with 'cat'?"

If she can name some words that rhyme, go to the next assessment.

If she can't, stop and work on Rhyming Activities in Chapter Seven.

Phonics Assessment

1. Show your child these words written on index cards:
   HAT, TED, WIN, DOG, CUP, LIKE, PLAY

2. Ask your child: "Can you tell me the sounds in this word?"

3. Listen to see if she can separate the sounds (H-A-T)

4. Then ask: "Can you read the word?"

If he knows the separate sounds, go to the next assessment.

If he can't separate the sounds in the words, then go to Phonics Activities in Chapter Eight.

Comprehension Assessment

Part I

1. Show your child this paragraph:

    The man has two feet but only one shoe. He needs to find the other shoe. Where is it? The man looks in his house. He finds his shoe in his bed. Now he has two shoes.

2. **Tell your child:** "Read this, and then tell me what it's about in your own words."

3. **If she** *can* **tell you what it's about,** go to the next assessment.

4. **If she** *can't* **tell you what it's about, you'll need to determine something very important:** Does she know that she doesn't understand?

If she doesn't know that she doesn't understand, then go to Chapter Eleven: Word Strategies and Reading Comprehension Strategies, Monitoring Meaning.

If she does know that she doesn't understand, then go to the section on Background Knowledge in Chapter Eleven.

Part II

1. Let your child choose a section in a book that he says he can read, **and ask him to read it aloud or silently.**

2. Follow along with him **as he reads it aloud, or read it silently after he does.**

3. Then ask your child questions to see if he knows what he just read. **Ask questions like "What happened?" and "Who is it about?"** that encourage him to use his own words to explain or answer.

If he didn't understand what he read, then you need to go to Chapter Eleven's Five Finger Test. Make sure he is picking a book that is "easy" or "just-right", starting with "easy" for now.

But if she understood what she read, then hooray! **Your child's issue is probably not that reading is too challenging.** Continue to the next assessment.

Tracking Assessment

1. **Sit with your child and follow along** while she reads aloud to you.

2. Does she skip words or lines? **Does she get lost?**

If so, she might have a tracking issue. Go to Chapter Three and read the Vision and Sight Section.

If not, go to the next assessment.

Fluency Assessment

1. Listen to your child read aloud.

2. Does he read haltingly, or without inflection? **Does he not pause at the ends of sentences (i.e., after periods)?**

If the answer to any of these is yes, go to Fluency Activities in Chapter Ten. If not, go to the next assessment.

Sight Word Assessment

1. Show your child the basic sight words **that are appropriate for his age, using one of the printable sight words lists.**

2. Does your child know the sight words for his age?

If not, work on learning all the age-appropriate sight words. For fun sight word games and activities, see Chapter Nine.

Product Recommendations
(To Make Reading Not Tricky)

Magnetic Letters

Pointers

Reader Strips™

See-Through Bookmarks

Star Alphabet Posters

Chapter Five: Too Sitty

My daughter is a mover—she's constantly in motion, even when she's sleeping. She hates sitting still for anything, including reading.

Some kids won't like reading if it goes hand in hand with sitting still.

Our active kids need us to think outside the chair.

Audiobooks

Listening to audiobooks isn't, technically, reading (as in reading print). You want your child to read, I understand. But it's okay to count audiobooks as reading—especially with active kids. Here's why:

1. Listening to an audiobook doesn't require sitting! A child can pace, wiggle, dance, roll around, whatever she needs to do. It's a great way to hook a mover and help her become a reader.

2. Your child needs to learn to love stories. Realizing that reading is the key to unlocking a fascinating story is hugely important in turning around reluctant readers.

3. Your child will build valuable knowledge about story elements—plot, conflict, beginning/middle/end, and so on. These can help your child understand what she reads and make more accurate predictions about stories.

4. You can ignite obsessions by listening to an audiobook series. Once your child gets interested, she might want to continue reading the series, read more by that author, or about that subject.

Don't forget, you can listen to audiobooks in the car, too!

Mealtime Stories

As a toddler and preschooler, my kinesthetic daughter wouldn't sit still to listen to an entire picture book story, so I'd follow her around to read her the entire book. That's when I started reading to her while she ate breakfast, lunch, snacks, and dinner. She was so busy eating that she became a captive audience (and she was trapped in her high chair!). Try making mealtime a story-reading time at your house.

The Walk-Read

Help your child perfect her walk-read . . . i.e. being able to walk while reading without incurring injury. (But please, safety first. And certainly don't allow this around stairs, uneven surfaces, or other dangerous terrain where eyes and mind need to be 100% on locomotion!)

Also, there is the stationary bike-read (I've seen this at innovative schools, and it looks fun!), the rocker/glider/hammock-read, the inside pod swing-read, and the on-the-floor-read.

Electronic Books

Some critics argue that e-books are too game-like. Maybe they are, but they do get reluctant readers reading. Personally, I count e-books as reading even if they include games. For specific e-book reading strategies, go to bit.ly/TdogMm on Imagination Soup.

Book Swap Party

Organize a party for kids to trade books they've read—but with a condition: they have to read the book in order to attend the swap. At the party, have each child give a short book talk (thumbs up, thumbs down, and why) so the other kids can know what it's about. Trade books using the White Elephant Gift Exchange rules (bit.ly/TEa8HZ).

Make a Book-Related Movie

Some kids are born performers. Use this passion to help them with their reading. Have them make a video of themselves reading aloud or giving a review/sharing their opinion of a book.

Websites like KidzVuz.com and Zui.com provide opportunities for kids to share videos with friends.

Reading Tent

Set up a tent or blanket fort. Add pillows, a flashlight or battery-powered lantern. Let your wiggly reader use it as a reading nook.

Short Nonfiction

Nonfiction books are great because they don't necessarily have to be read sequentially (that is, from beginning to end). Often, your child can dip into them wherever she likes—reading just the chapter on mummies in a book about Ancient Egypt, if mummies are what she loves. Then, if she wants, she can read the chapters on pharaohs, on how the pyramids were built, and so on. Jumping around a book can be perfect for our most active readers! For a list of engaging nonfiction titles, go to Chapter Twelve.

Piles of Books

Strange as it sounds, I sneak around the house and leave piles of library books for my kids to discover. The adventure of discovering them makes the books so tempting, neither child can resist the urge to investigate. Often one or two books will "take," and my kids will sit down with that book and read.

Picture Books

Picture books should be part of your reading diet. Picture books are great for kids with shorter attention spans because there's so much to engage them: they're rich with vocabulary, the illustrations provide extra context to the story, and they offer amazing stories. As such, they develop knowledge through a multi-sensory experience. And contrary to what you might think, picture books are not easy reading: many are written at a 4th to 5th grade reading level. To get you started, check out School Library Journal's list of top picture books (bit.ly/XPbXXp).

Product Recommendations
(To Make Reading Not Sitty)

My Magical Cushion

Chew Stixx

Modern Ball Chair

Headlamp

IPod Touch **(load it up with audiobooks)**

Headphones

Indoor Swing

Mind Putty

Fold-and-Go Trampoline

Chapter Six: Favorit
Alphabet Acti

Alphabet activities develop a child's knowledge and love of letters. If your child is a beginning reader, you'll want to be sure that she knows the alphabet, both upper and lower case.

Browse through and experiment,
finding the activities your child likes best.

Buried Letters

Hide plastic letters in the sandbox or dirt for your young child to discover. If your child can spell his name or can spell simple words, hide those letters and help your child build the words once he finds them.

Alphabet Sort

Sort alphabet letters in different ways: by curvy or straight lines, by colors, by letters in the child's name, or by any other criteria.

Alphabet Songs

Sing the traditional ABC song periodically throughout the day—while brushing teeth, washing hands, or during a walk.

Chalk Alphabet and "Alphabet People"

Use sidewalk chalk to write the alphabet and draw funny-looking people using alphabet letters.

Alphabet Puzzles

Alphabet puzzles are engaging, hands-on practice for kids.

Letter Scavenger Hunt

Cut out large letters from magazines. Glue them one by one onto index cards. Hide them around the house for your kids to find. You can up the ante for older readers by challenging them to find all the letters that spell a specific word. Add a magnifying glass for more searching fun.

Letters with Play-Doh, Pipe Cleaners, Wikki Stix, or LEGOs

Help your child use any "bendy" and "build-y" materials to make her own alphabet letters.

I Spy

Look around the house for items that start with specific letters. Start in the kitchen: "I spy with my little eye something that starts with the letter B." (Possibilities in the kitchen include: bananas, bottle, box, bucket, burner, bubbles, bags, bin, bib.)

Name Puzzles

To help your child learn the letters in his name, write his name on a sheet of paper or cardboard and cut the sheet into puzzle pieces. Help him put his name back together.

Salt, Shaving Cream, or Sand Writing

Use as many tactile materials as you can to practice writing letters. It helps your child to learn about letters (and thus reading) through all of his senses: seeing them, hearing them, saying them, and holding/touching/tracing/cutting them.

Alphabet Game on the Road

In the car or on the bus or subway, look for specific letters on signs or ads. Try to find all the As, or Ds, or whatever letter you're practicing. Older kids can do this as a timed exercise while you wait for a traffic light to change, or between subway or bus stops.

Alphabet Hopscotch

Write the letters of the alphabet in the hopscotch squares instead of numbers. Play by saying the letters when you land on them.

DIY Alphabet Collections

Select a container (bag, box, or jar) and designate it to hold items beginning with a particular letter. Help your child find things that start with that letter to put in the container. Your child can draw or cut out pictures of things too big to put in the container, and could even decorate the container with drawings and cut-outs of the designated letter.

Alphabet Rocks

Help your child make her own alphabet by painting each letter on rocks.

Alphabet Collage Books

Make your own alphabet book. Use blank books or sheets of paper, designating one page for each letter. Find pictures in magazines that match each letter. For example, you might cut out and glue down pictures like these for the letter "c": cat, cup, coffee, cow, or candle.

Online Alphabet Games

Alphabetical Adventure

Alphabet Whack-a-Mole

The ABC's Zoo Learning Game

Alphabet Product Recommendations

ABC Cookies Goodie Games™

ABC Punch Out Blocks

Alphabet Blocks

Alphabet Letters

    Foam

    Magnetic

    Foam and Magnetic

Alphabet Music

Alphabet Pebbles

Alphabet Puzzle

Alphabet Soup Sorters

Alphabet Stamps

Aquadoodle

Fridge Phonics

Lacing Alphabet

Letter Matching Game

Magnadoodle

POP for Letters™ Game

Purpllinker

Smart Snacks® ABC Lacing Sweets

Wikki-Stix Alphabet Cards

Wipe Clean Letters

Chapter Seven: Favorite Rhyming Activities

To read, children need to be able to rhyme. **If a child knows how to rhyme with the word** hat**, she can then read** bat, mat, cat and rat.

Sing Rhyming Songs

Down By the Bay

Miss Mary Mack

Baa, Baa, Black Sheep

One, Two, Buckle My Shoe

Row, Row, Row Your Boat

Song Variations:

1. Change the rhyming words in the songs.
2. Start all the words with the same letter. Sing *"Down By the Bay"* using the letter "M" to start the words so it becomes *"Mown My the May."*

Rhyme Every Day

Practice rhyming every day. Look around and find an object. Say, "Let's try to find things that rhyme with *[the object]*." Nonsense words are great, too—be silly and playful!

Magnetic Letter Rhymes

Use foam or magnetic letters to make a word. See if you can change a few letters to make a new word that rhymes with it.

Example: Spell out the word "jump". Change the "j" to a "p" to make "pump". If you take away the "p" can you add another letter to make a new word? This is a perfect time to introduce Word Families, a group of words with the same letter-sound combinations. **(Lists on Book-Love.net.)**

Jump and Rhyme

This is a great game for kids who are always on the go. Do jumping jacks (or jump on a trampoline, or jump rope) while you rhyme words.

Which Doesn't Belong?

Say three words—two that rhyme and one that doesn't. Ask, "Which word doesn't belong?"

Example: hat, mat, sandwich

20 Questions

One player thinks of a word and provides a 2-part clue, including a rhyme hint: "I'm thinking of a word that rhymes with lock, and it's something that you wear." The other players ask questions that can be answered by a "yes" or "no". Example questions: "Is it alive?" "Do you wear it every day?" "Is it bigger than me?"

Online Rhyming Games

Super Grover's The Nick of Rhyme

Sesame Street: Rhyming Day

Rhyming Games **(PBS Kids)**

"Six Games for Reading" **by Bank Street College of Education**
What's in the [Work] Box? Handmade Word Family Game

Rhyming Product Recommendations

Eeboo Rhyming Word Puzzle Pairs

Fingerplays and Rhymes in a Jar®

My Book of Rhyming Words

Nir! Games: Rhyming War

Picture Rhymes Concentration

Really Good Rhyming Kit

Rhyming Bingo

Rhyming Marks the Spot™ Floor Game

Rhyming Puzzle Cards

Rhyming Words Workbook (Hooked on Phonics)

The Complete Book and CD Set of Rhymes, Songs, Poems, Fingerplays, and Chants

Word Building Game Chunks

Zingo! Bingo with a Zing

Chapter Eight: Phonics and Favorite Phonics Activities

Letters all have sounds. A reader must know the sounds for each letter or combination of letters and be able to blend them to read a word. That's phonics.

If your child is struggling to read the sounds in words, he is having trouble with what's called decoding. Phonics helps kids decode the letter-sound relationships and put those together to make words.

To help your child with phonics, you need a bit more information. See which of the sounds below she knows or doesn't know. You can find out by listening to her read.

Vowel Sounds: a, e, i, o, u and sometimes y

Short Vowels

When a vowel is followed by a consonant, it is short.

Examples: **cat, jet, hit, pot, but**

Long Vowels

Magic e! If a short word ends with an e, most often the vowel is long and says its name, and the e is silent.

Examples: **same, here, like, home, tube**

Diphthong

No, this is not what you call a bad driver! It's what you call two vowels that appear together, and make one sound.

Examples: **oo, ou, ie, ay, oy, ue, au**

Vowels Under the Influence of R

When a vowel is followed by the letter r, it's called an r-controlled vowel because the r affects the sound.

Examples: **the /ar/ sound in car** or the **/ir/ sound in spider**

Consonants

Consonant Blends

Take a few consonants, put them together, blend, and read!

Examples: **bl-, st-**

Consonant Digraphs

Some consonants are so crazy that together they make new sounds.

Examples: **ph-, ch-, sh-, th-**

Word Families

The term Word Family refers to a group of words with the same letter-sound combinations. You'll find Word Families and rhyming go hand in hand. See lists of Word Families on Book-Love.net.

Examples: **the -ill family: bill, mill, hill, fill (etc.)**

Phonics Activities and Games

When you play phonics activities and games with your child, focus on one sound or word family at a time. When your child has mastered that sound or word family, then move to the next.

Make a Word

On index cards, write letters or letter combinations, one per card. Put the cards into a hat, jar, or bag and shake them up. Take turns picking a card and thinking of a word containing those letters.

Example: If you draw a card with "ph", you could say the word "phone."

For printable sound cards visit Book-Love.net.

Sound Bingo

Print out these word family bingo cards from Preschool Universe at bit.ly/VzWxcb. The object of the game is to cover a row or achieve a blackout.

Alphabets to Words

Pull out your alphabet magnets or blocks. Have your child make as many words as he can using the letter sound you're working on.

I Spy Beginning and Ending Sounds

Say, "I spy with my little eye something that begins with a _____ [insert sound here]." Or, "I spy with my little eye something that ends with a _____ [insert sound here]."

Letter-Sound Hopscotch

Write the letters of the alphabet in the hopscotch squares instead of numbers. Play by saying the letter sounds when you land on one.

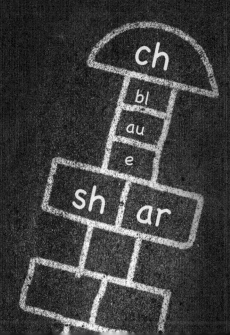

Syllable Jars

Label five jars one through five. On index cards, write a word on each card that your child knows or is practicing. Say the words and help your child clap out the syllables in the word. Sort the words into the jars based on the number of syllables they have.

Sounds Scavenger Hunt

On each of ten index cards, write a digraph or blend. Hide the cards around the house. Give your child clues for finding each card. When she finds a card, she can say the sound and keep the card. Give her a small prize for finding all ten.

Words Around the House

Look for things around the house your child can label with a sticky note. Help her write the word and stick it to the object.

Word Family Game

Use these printable word family flash cards on Apples 4 the Teacher at bit.ly/OZyEqz as a resource.

Word Family Wheels

Try these printable word family word wheels on Super Teacher Worksheets at bit.ly/X9lSHT.

DIY Word Family Sliders

Print out the word family labels to make this easy flash card review game. Print out the word family labels to make this easy flash card review game from Make, Take & Teach from bit.ly/Tdy8pe.

Free Phonics Videos

Syllable Lesson Video **(Learning Games for Kids)**

Transformer H (The Electric Company, sung by Ne-Yo)

Silent E (The Electric Company, sung by James Iglehart)

Bossy R (The Electric Company, sung by Veronica Jackson)

Between the Lions **on PBS Kids**

Who Let the Letters Out? **(Dr. Jean)**

Visit Book-Love.net for video links.

Phonics Product Recommendations

Link 26

Montessori Phonetic Object Box

Montessori Phonetic Reading Blocks

Phonics iPad Apps

POP for Word Families Card Game

Reading Rods

Sandpaper Letters

Snatch-It

Spell It

Toobaloo®

Word Families Slide and Learn™

Chapter Nine: Sight Words Lists and Favorite Activities

You've probably heard of sight words. These are words that kids need to know to be successful readers. **But they're words kids can't sound out. Children need to learn these words by sight.**

Dolch and Fry are the two sight word lists that most schools use. I'm including the Dolch sight words for this book. However, feel free to try the Fry sight words as well. There is overlap but Fry's list is longer.

Sight Word Lists

Go to Book-Love.net for printable Dolch Sight Words: Pre-Primer, Primer, 1st Grade, 2nd Grade, 3rd Grade.

Sight Word Bingo

Make a Bingo game using the sight words your child needs to learn. Use a free online Bingo board maker to input your words, such as the 3x3 or 4x4 board makers on Tools for Educators (www.toolsforeducators.com/bingo/), or the many types of Bingo cards you can make using Print Bingo (print-bingo.com/).

Fridge Sight Words

Use magnetic alphabet letters to practice spelling sight words on the refrigerator.

Search and Find Sight Words (in books)

Get a favorite book and see if your child can find all of places where [a specific sight word] appears.

Stamp the Sight Word

Use alphabet stamps to make your own sight word flashcards.

Sight Word Hangman

Play Hangman with sight words.

Sight Word Go Fish

Make your own sight word Go Fish game. Make 20 pairs of sight words. Play to get pairs.

Sight Words Memory

Use the cards from Go Fish to play memory match up. Each player turns over two cards. The object is to match the two cards. When you do, you can keep both cards. The winner is the player with the most cards.

Sight Word Wall

When your child learns a new sight word, add it to a designated "Word Wall" of words he knows! Write the words on sticky notes, index cards, or construction paper.

Sight Word Scavenger Hunt

Write a sight word on each of ten index cards. Hide them around the house. Give your child clues for finding each card. When she finds a card, she can keep it if she knows the word. If she finds and knows all ten words, she wins a small prize.

Sight Word Hopscotch

Write sight words in the hopscotch squares instead of numbers. Play by saying the word when you land on each one.

Sight Word Flip Book

Buy a book of spiral-bound index cards. On the first page, write one sight word your child needs to learn. Practice that word until your child has mastered it. Then flip to the next card and write another word. Repeat.

Sight Word Product Recommendations

Alphabet Stamps

Bananagrams

Storymaker Magnetic Poetry Kit

Magnetic Sight Words

POP for Sight Words Game

Sight Word Books: Level 1: Reproducible Readers to Share at School and Home

Sight Word Bingo

Sight Word Flash Cards

Sight Word Plastic Tiles

Sight Word String Up Set

uKloo Treasure Hunt

What's Gnu?

Zingo! Bingo with a Zing

Chapter Ten: Favorite Fluency Activities

Fluency is the ability to read smoothly, in the way a person talks, with appropriate breaks and inflections for punctuation (such as periods and question marks).

Fluency requires a reader to be able to decode words, pronounce them, and read them without hesitation. Reading fluently is essential to comprehension **because it helps the words enter short-term memory, resulting in reading comprehension.**

Conversely, a halting reader will have forgotten most of the sentence by the time she's finished reading it, since earlier parts of the sentence are no longer in her short-term memory.

Echo Reading

Read aloud the words to a story and have your child echo your words just after you read them, trying to copy your inflection.

Exaggerate Punctuation

When reading aloud, exaggerate the punctuation by counting out loud or silently.

Periods = count to three.

Commas = count to one.

Questions = make your voice higher at the end of the sentence.

Exclamations = get loud!

Silly Voices

Practice reading aloud using silly voices:

- a "fancy" person
- a robot
- a monster
- a baby
- a sad person
- a fast talker
- a slow talker
- a whisperer
- a loud talker
- a southern accent
- [fill in your own!]

Poetry Slam

Choose a poem and practice reading it aloud. Then memorize it and perform it with dramatic flair, as if you were in a poetry slam. Get the whole family involved in this one!

Audio Books

Listen to an audio book while following along in the print book. Use a finger or bookmark to track the words.

Recorded Reading

Record your child reading aloud from a favorite book. Then make the recording more interesting by adding sound effects and music.

Fluency Product Recommendations

Between the Lions Stories

Easi-Speak™ USB Recorder

Fluency Timer

Now I'm Reading Plays: Three Little Pigs

Silly Sentences

Reading Plus

Raz-Kids

Chapter Eleven

Word Strategies and Reading Comprehension Strategies

Good readers use specific strategies;
strategies that all readers can learn and use.
This goes for reading individual words and reading sentences for comprehension.

Beyond Sounding It Out:
Five Strategies That Can Help Read Words

If your child comes to a word she doesn't know, telling her to "sound it out" doesn't always work. Here's what else you can say and some additional strategies you can teach.

1. Are There Picture Clues?

Tell your child, "Look at the pictures. Do the pictures help you figure out the word?"

2. What are the Beginning and Ending Sounds?

Help your child figure out the beginning sound of a word first. Often that's enough to use the clues in the sentence around it (context clues) to figure it out.

3. Are There Small Words Inside the Big Word?

See if your child can see any small words that he already knows, inside the larger word.

Example: The word "begin" has two small words: "be" and "in". Then, just make the "g" sound in the middle!

4. Can You Chunk It?

See if your child can break the word into several chunks. Then, put the chunks together.

Example: The word "backpack" can be chunked into "back" and "pack".

5. Skip It, Read the Rest of the Sentence, Come Back to It

Your child may be able to figure out the word after she reads the entire sentence. This can help prevent your child's feeling stuck when she encounters a word she doesn't know.

Five Finger Test for Book Selection

Open the book to any page in the middle. Read the page. For every word you don't know, hold up one finger. If you have zero fingers up, the book is an easy book for you. If you have between one and five fingers, the book is "just-right"! High-five yourself. A just-right book is a book you can read and comprehend. If you have six or more fingers up, the book is too challenging. Save it for later.

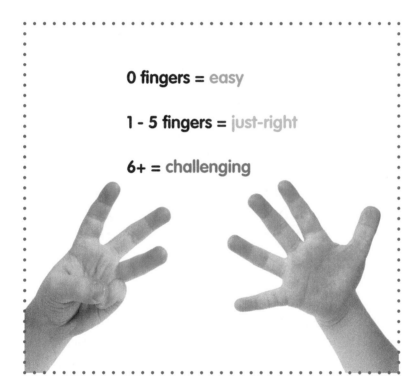

0 fingers = easy

1 - 5 fingers = just-right

6+ = challenging

Reading Comprehension Strategies:
Understanding What You Read

Your children will become better readers, readers who comprehend what they are reading, when they use these research-based strategies.[6] It takes practice to get the hang of these reading strategies. Don't worry if your child needs weeks or months to develop them. Every year, a child can continue to deepen her ability to use the strategies.

1. Monitor Understanding
"I know / don't know what's happening."

Children must know when they're confused and when they understand. For some kids, this isn't intuitive. Parents, we can help them check in with their brains to ask, do I understand or is this confusing.

> **Practice:** Stop and ask, "Hmm, does this make sense? What is happening here?" Ask and answer your own questions. Then help your child do it, too.

2. Connect to the Book
"That reminds me of . . . "

When we read, we put ourselves in the characters' shoes, compare the characters to people we know and other stories we read. That's using background knowledge.

> **Practice:** While you read, make connections out loud so your child can hear your connections. Ask your child to share his connections. Help him think of some if he can't.

3. Determine What's Important
"Is that interesting or important?"

Good readers know the difference between what is important and what's interesting.

> **Practice:** When you're reading, talk about interesting things (a blue dress) and important things (the main character is Jack). Ask your child if she thinks [any part of the story] is interesting or important. Talk about how you can tell the difference.

4. Make Pictures in Your Head
"Can you see the movie in your head?"

Good readers use all their senses to imagine the story. We visualize what's happening, and use all the sensory details the author gives us—hearing, tasting, feeing, smelling—to create this imagine in our minds.

> **Practice:** When you're reading, close your eyes and talk about the picture in your head. Ask your child to do the same.

5. Ask Questions
"I wonder . . . "

Good readers think of questions as they read like "I wonder why the character just did _____?" or "I wonder what will happen?" Questions help your child make inferences (see below) and predictions.

> **Practice:** As you read, stop and ask questions out loud. This shows your child how to question. Ask your child if he has any questions. Help him if he doesn't.

6. Make Inferences (Draw Conclusions)

"I can make a good guess using the clues the author gives me . . . "

An inference is when you figure out what isn't said directly.

Example: if you read about a wet boy in a bathing suit carrying a towel, you can make an inference that he just went swimming. Or if you read that someone was scowling, you can infer that she might be feeling worried, mad, or upset.

> **Practice**: Help your child to make predictions about what will happen next in the story. You say a really silly prediction first that makes no sense. Then, together make a better prediction using what you've already read in the story. Talk about how the author gives us clues to help us make good predictions.

7. Synthesize information

"If I put together all the information, I can now say that _____."

This high-level thinking strategy combines information a reader has comprehended from reading as well as a personal spin on it. It's kind of like a summary plus your own analysis. (Imagine synthesizing all those parenting books you've read!)

> **Practice**: Read several books by the same author or about the same topic. Use what you learned from the different books to synthesize what you now know about either the author or the topic.

Comprehension Product Recommendations

Hidden Hints™ Mystery Word Game

Capture the Flag: Reading Comprehension Game

Book Mission Kit

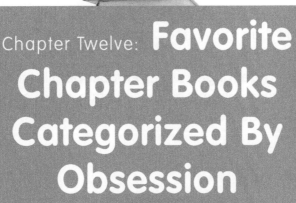

Chapter Twelve: **Favorite Chapter Books Categorized By Obsession**

To get started, find the category your child likes. Click on the title and you'll go to the book information on Barnes and Noble.

Look for the **"Age range"** under **Product Details** (scroll down) to give you more information. These lists contain a range of easy readers, early chapter books, and chapter books.

Adventure Books

39 Clues by Various Authors

Akimbo and the Crocodile Man by Alexander McCall Smith

Alex Rider Series by Anthony Horowitz

Andrew Lost Series by J.C. Greenburg

Capital Mysteries Series by Ron Roy

Chet Gecko Mystery Series by Bruce Hale

Commander Toad and the Voyage Home by Jane Yolen

Doyle and Fossey Science Detectives Series by Michele Torrey

Flat Stanley Collection by Jeff Brown

Frankie Pickle Series by Eric Wight

Ghost Knight by Cornelia Funke

Holes by Louis Sachar

How to Train Your Dragon Series by Cressida Cowell

Igraine the Brave by Cornelia Funke

Ivy and Bean Series by Annie Barrows

Max Spaniel Series by David Catrow

Milo and Jazz Mysteries by Lewis B. Montgomery

Miraculous Journey of Edward Tulane by Kate DiCamillo

Nancy Clancy by Jane O'Connor

NERDS Series by Michael Buckley

Pippi Longstocking by Astrid Lindgren

Secret Agent: Jack Stalwart Series by Elizabeth Singer Hunt

The Emerald Atlas Series by John Stephens

The Genius Files Series by Dan Gutman

The Incorrigible Children of Ashton Place Series
by Maryrose Wood

The Littles by John Lawrence Peterson

The Mysterious Benedict Society Series
by Trenton Lee Stewart

The Name of this Book Is a Secret Series
by Pseudonymous Bosch

Thief Lord by Cornelia Funke

Alphabet Books (Picture Books)

A is for Angry by Sandra Boynton

A Long Piece of String by William Wondriska

Dogs ABCs by Connie Sharar

ABC3D by Marion Bataille

Al Pha's Bet by Amy Krouse Rosenthal

Alphabeasties and Other Amazing Types by Sharon Werner

Alphabet Mystery by Audrey Wood

Alphabet Under Construction by Denise Fleming

AlphaOops! The Day Z Went First by Alethea Kontis

Animalia by Graeme Base

Backseat A-B-See by Maria Van Lieshout

Basher: ABC Kids by Simon Basher

Chicka Chicka Boom Boom
by Bill Martin, Jr., and John Archambault

Eric Carle's ABCs by Eric Carle

I Spy A to Z: A Book of Picture Riddles by Jean Marzollo

I Spy: Alphabet in Art by Lucy Micklethwait

LMNO Peas by Keith Baker

Poor Puppy and Bad Kitty by Nick Bruel

Puddle's ABC by Holly Hobbie

The Absolutely Awful Alphabet by Mordicai Gerstein

The Alphabet from A to Y with Bonus Letter Z!
by Steve Martin and Roz Chast

The Book of Shadowboxes: A Story of the ABC's
by Laura L. Seeley

Z is for Moose by Kelly Bingham
(illustrated by Paul O. Zelinsky)

Animal Books

A Mouse Called Wolf by Dick King-Smith

Aggie Gets Lost by Lori Ries

Charlotte's Web by E.B. White

DC Super-Pets Series by Various Authors

Daisy Dawson Series by Steve Voake

Frog and Toad Are Friends by Arnold Lobel

Geronimo Stilton Series by Geronimo Stilton

Ghost Dog Secrets by Peg Kehert

Horse Crazy Series by Alison Lester

Jigsaw Pony by Jessie Haas

J.J. Tully Series by Doreen Cronin

Marley: A Dog Like No Other by John Grogan

Mason Dixon: Pet Disasters by Claudia Mills

Mercy Watson Series by Kate DiCamillo

Mrs. Frisby and the Rats of NIMH by Robert C. O'Brien

National Geographic Kids: And More True Stories of Amazing Animals Heroes by National Geographic Kids

Horse Diaries Series by Whitney Sanderson

Pet Fairies (Rainbow Magic) by Daisy Meadows

Puppy Place Series by Ellen Miles

Rainbow Street Shelter Series by Wendy Orr

Saddle Wise Series by Inda Schaenen

Tale of Despereaux by Kate DiCamillo

The Cricket in Times Square by George Selden

The Buddy Files by Dori Hillestad Butler

The Mouse and the Motorcycle by Beverly Cleary

The One and Only Ivan by Katherine Applegate

World According to Humphrey by Betty G. Birney

Art/Artist Books

A Nest for Celeste by Henry Cole

A Single Shard by Linda Sue Park

Chasing Vermeer by Blue Balliett

Lives of the Artists: Masterpieces, Messes (and What the Neighbors Thought) by Kathleen Krull

Masterpiece by Elise Broach

Noonie's Masterpiece by Lisa Railsback

Storybook Art: Hands-on Art for Children in the Style of 100 Great picture Book Authors by MaryAnn F. Kohl, Jean Potter and Rebecca Van Slyke

The Calder Game by Blue Balliett

The Strange Case of the Origami Yoda by Tom Angleberger

Wonderstruck by Brian Selznick

Banned or Challenged Books

A Wrinkle in Time by Madeline L'Engle

Anne Frank: The Diary of a Young Girl by Anne Frank

Bridge to Terabithia by Katherine Paterson

Flowers for Algernon by Daniel Keyes

Forever by Judy Blume

I Know Why the Caged Bird Sings by Maya Angelou

The Giver by Lois Lowry

The Harry Potter Series by J. K. Rowling

The Hunger Games by Suzanne Collins

The Lord of the Rings Series by J. R. R. Tolkien

Books with Movies

A Series of Unfortunate Events by Lemony Snicket

Babe: The Gallant Pig by Dick King-Smith

Because of Winn-Dixie by Kate DiCamillo

Charlie and the Chocolate Factory by Roald Dahl

Chronicles of Narnia by C. S. Lewis

Coraline by Neil Gaiman

Ella Enchanted by Gail Carson Levine

Guardians of Ga'Hoole by Kathryn Lasky

Harriet the Spy by Louise Fitzhugh

Harry Potter by J. K. Rowling

Hoot by Carl Hiaasen

Hotel for Dogs by Lois Duncan

How to Train Your Dragon by Cressida Cowell

Judy Moody and the Not Bummer Summer by Megan McDonald

Matilda by Roald Dahl

Mr. Popper's Penguins by Richard and Florence Atwater

Mrs. Frisby and the Rats of NIHM by Robert C. O'Brien

Nancy Drew Series by Carolyn Keene

Nim's Island by Wendy Orr and Kerry Millard

Percy Jackson and the Olympians Series by Rick Riordan

Peter Pan by J. M. Barrie

Pippi Longstocking by Astrid Lindgren

Ramona by Beverly Cleary

Stuart Little by E. B. White

The Baby Sitter's Club by Ann M. Martin

The Borrowers by Mary Norton

The Diary of a Wimpy Kid by Jeff Kinney

The Invention of Hugo Cabret by Brian Selznick

The Lorax by Dr. Seuss

The Night at the Museum by Milan Trenc

The Princess Diaries Series by Meg Cabot

The Secret Garden by Frances Hodgson Burnett

The Spiderwick Chronicles by Tony DiTerlizzi and Holly Black

The Tale of Despereaux by Kate DiCamillo

The Wonderful Wizard of Oz by L. Frank Baum

Funny Books

A Whole Nother Story by Dr. Cuthbert Soup

A Year Down Yonder by Richard Peck

Bad Kitty Series by Nick Bruel

Big Nate Series by Lincoln Peirce

Boom by Mark Haddon

Diary of a Wimpy Kid Series by Jeff Kinney

Dr. Proctor's Fart Powder Series by Jo Nesbo

Dragonbreath Series by Ursula Vernon

EllRay Jakes Series by Sally Warner

Encyclopedia of Immaturity by the Editors of Klutz

Franny K. Stein Series by Jim Benton

Freckle Juice by Judy Blume

Frindle & The Landry News by Andrew Clements

Got Cake? Rotten School #13 by R. L. Stein

How to Eat Fried Worms by Thomas Rockwell

How to Train Your Dragon by Cressida Cowell

Joey Pigza Series by Jack Gantos

Knucklehead: Tall Tales & Mostly True Stories of Growing Up Scieszka by Jon Scieszka

Lulu and the Brontosaurus by Judith Viorst

Lunch Lady Series by Jarrett Krosoczka

Magic Pickle Series by Scott Morse

Melonhead by Katy Kelly

Moxy Maxwell Does Not Love Writing Thank-you Notes by Peggy Gifford

Mudshark by Gary Paulsen

My Weird School Series by Dan Gutman

NERDS Series by Michael Buckley

Raymond and Graham Series by Mike Knudson

Seriously Silly Stories Series by Laurence Anholt

Shredderman Series by Wendelin Van Draanen

Spaceheadz by Jon Scieszka

Stink Series by Megan McDonald

Sweet Farts Series by Raymond Bean

The Misadventures of Inspector Moustachio by Wayne Madsen

The BFG by Roald Dahl

The Dunderheads by Paul Fleischman

The Enormous Egg by Oliver Butterworth

The Problem with the Puddles by Kate Feiffer

Vordak the Incomprehensible Series by Vordak T.

Wayside School Series by Louis Sachar

Friendship Books

Alvin Ho: Allergic to Camping, Hiking, and Other Natural Disasters by Lenore Look

American Girl Today Series by Various Authors

Andy Shane Hero at Last by Jennifer Richard

Anna Hibiscus Series by Atinuke

Beyond Lucky by Sarah Aronson

Charlotte's Web by E. B. White

Clementine by Sara Pennypacker

Frindle by Andrew Clements

Gooney Bird Series by Lois Lowry

Heart of a Samurai by Margi Preus

Henry and Mudge Series by Cynthia Rylant

Holes by Louis Sachar

How to Eat Fried Worms by Thomas Rockwell

Ivy and Bean Series by Annie Barrows

Judy Moody Series by Megan McDonald

Kylie Jean Series by M. Peschke

Lawn Boy by Gary Paulsen

Dyamonde Daniel Series by Nikki Grimes

Marty McGuire by Kate Messner

Pain and the Great One Series by Judy Blume

Ramona by Beverly Cleary

Roxie and the Hooligans by Phyllis Reynolds Naylor

The Friendship Doll by Kirby Larson

The Hundred Dresses by Eleanor Estes

The Penderwicks Series by Jeanne Birdsall

The Popularity Papers Series by Amy Ignatow

Wonder by R .J. Palacio

Zeke Meeks Series by D. L. Green

Zigzag Kids Series by Patricia Reilly Giff

Graphic Novels (Cartoons)

Amelia Rules! Series by Jimmy Gownley

Amulet Series by Kazu Kibuishi

Artemis Fowl: The Graphic Novel by Eoin Colfer

Avatar: The Last Airbender Series by various authors

Babymouse Series by Jennifer Holm and Matthew Holm

Barron's Graphic Classics by Various Authors

Benjamin Bear in Fuzzy Thinking (Toon) by Philippe Coudray

Benny and Penny (Toon) Series by Geoffrey Hayes

Binky, the Space Cat Adventures Series by Ashley Spires

Bone Series by Jeff Smith

Dragonbreath Series by Ursula Vernon

Fashion Kitty Series by Charise Mericle Harper

Giants Beware by Jorge Aguirre

Guinea Pig, Pet Shop Private Eye Series by Colleen AF Venable

Little Mouse Gets Ready (Toon) by Jeff Smith

Little Vampire by Joann Sfar

Lunch Lady Series by Jarrett Krosoczka

Magic Pickle Series by Scott Morse

Mal and Chad Series by Stephan McCranie

Missile Mouse: The Star Crusher by Jake Parker

Nina in That Makes Me Mad by Hilary Knight

Ninjago Graphic Novels Series by Greg Farshtey

Nursery Rhyme Comics: 50 Timeless Rhymes from 50 Celebrated Cartoonists by Various Authors

Owly Series by Andy Runton

Rapunzel's Revenge by Dean Hale, Shannon Hale and Nathan Hale

Rick and Rack and the Great Outdoors (Balloon Toons) by Ethan Long

Sidekicks by Dan Santat

Silly Lilly Series (Toon) by Agnes Rosenstiehl

Stinky (Toon) by Eleanor Davis

Alex Rider Series: The Graphic Novel by Antony Johnson and Anthony Horowitz

The Adventures of Tintin Series by Herge

The Olympians Series by George O'Connor

The Secret Science Alliance and the Copycat Crook by Eleanor Davis

Warriors: SkyClan and the Strangers Series by Erin Hunter

Zita the Space Girl Series by Ben Hatke

Zoe and Robot, Let's Pretend (Balloon Toons) by Ryan Sias

Magazine
Toddlers

Babybug

Preschoolers

Click
Wild Animal Baby

Early Elementary

Ask
Big Backyard
Chirp
Humpty Dumpty
National Geographic Little Kids
Turtle

Elementary

American Girl

Boys' Quest

ChickADee

Discovery Girls

Jack and Jill

Owl

Ranger Rick

Sports Illustrated Kids

Yum Food and Fun for Kids

Zoobooks

Magic Books

Animorphs by Katherine Applegate

Artemis Fowl by Eoin Colfer

Dragon Slayers' Academy Series by Kate McMullan

Earwig and the Witch by Diana Wynne Jones

Ella Enchanted by Gail Carson Levine

Emily Windsnap Series by Liz Kessler

Gregor The Overlander Series by Suzanne Collins

Beastologist Series by R. L. LaFevers

Fablehaven Series by Brandon Mull

Harry Potter Series by J. K. Rowling

Inkheart Series by Cornelia Funke

Kingdom Keepers Series by Ridley Pearson

Magic Tree House Series by Mary Pope Osborne

Magical Animal Fairies Series by Daisy Meadows

Matilda by Roald Dahl

Odd and the Frost Giants by Neil Gaiman

Percy Jackson and the Olympians Series by Rick Riordan

Starcatchers Series by Dave Barry and Ridley Pearson

Sea of Trolls Series by Nancy Farmer

Storybound by Marissa Burt

The Doll People Series by Ann M. Martin

The Land of Stories by Chris Colfer

The Lion, the Witch and the Wardrobe by C. S. Lewis

The Secret of Droon Series by Tony Abbott

The Sisters Eight Series by Lauren Baratz-Logsted

The Strange Case of the Origami Yoda Series by Tom Angleberger

The Toys Go Out by Emily Jenkins

Time Warp Trio Series by Jon Scieszka

Tuesdays at the Castle by Jessica Day George

Winterling by Sarah Prineas

Non-Fiction Books

13 Planets: The Latest View of the Solar System (National Geographic Kids) by David A. Aguilar

Encyclopedia of Immaturity Series by Klutz

Fold Me a Poem by Kristine O'Connel George

Harry Potter Film Wizardry by Brain Sibley

Harry Potter Page to Screen by Bob McCabe

Illusionology Series by Various Authors

Jokelopedia: The Biggest, Best, Silliest, Dumbest, Dopiest Joke Book Ever by Ilana Weitzman, Eva Blank, and Rosanne Green

Kids' Fun and Healthy Cookbook by Nicola Graimes

Laugh Out Loud Jokes for Kids by Rob Elliott

LEGO Harry Potter: Characters of the Magical World by DK Publishing

LEGO Star Wars Character Encyclopedia by Hannah Dolan

National Geographic Kids Almanac by National Geographic Kids

National Geographic Kids Ultimate U.S. Road Trip Atlas

Oh, Yuck! The Encyclopedia of Everything Nasty by Joy Masoff

Ripley's Believe it or Not Series by Ripley's Inc. and Ripley's Entertainment Inc.

Star Wars: The Complete Visual Dictionary by David West Reynolds, James Luceno and Ryder Windham

Swords by Ben Boos

The Day-Glo Brothers: The Trues Story of Bob and Joe Switzer's Bright Ideas and Brilliant Colors by Chris Barton

The Way Things Work Series by David Macaulay

The Worst-Case Scenario Survive-o-Pedia by David Borgenicht

TIME for Kids Big Book of Why: 1,001 Facts Kids Want to Know by John Perritano

Treasury of Greek Mythology: Classic Stories of Gods, Goddesses, Heroes & Monsters by Donna Jo Napoli and Christina Balit

Weird But True Series by National Geographic Kids

Who Was? Biography Series by Various Authors

You Wouldn't Want to Be Series by Various Authors

Phonics Books and Early Readers

A Day on the Farm by Karen Walberg

Ants in her Pants by Paul Orshoski

Around Town (LEGO DK Readers) by Victoria Taylor

Bob Books, Set 1, 2, 3, 4 by Bobby Lyn Maslen

Bob Books: Sight Words Kindergarten, First Grade by Lynn Maslen Kertell

Fat Cat on a Mat by Phil Roxbee Cox

Fly Guy Series by Tedd Arnold

Hooked on Phonics Learn to Read Kindergarten

Hooked on Phonics Learn to Read 1st Grade

Ice Cream for Breakfast by Erica Farber

Learn to Read by The Starfall Team

LEGO Ninjago Reader Series by Tracy West

Little Miss Muffet by Jeffrey B. Fuerst

Meet Our Pets by John Serrano

National Geographic Readers Series by Various Authors

Pal and Sal by R.A. Herman

Pinkalicious (I Can Read) Series by Victoria Kann

Miss Kangaroo's Pouch by Karen Walberg

Sam Sheep Can't Sleep (Usborne Phonics Readers) by Phil Roxbee Cox

The Big Fat Cow that Goes Kapow by Andy Griffiths

The Magic Porridge Pot (Usborne First Reading) retold by Rosie Dickins

The Neat Pig (Read it, Write it, Draw it) by Nora Gaydos

There Was a Crooked Man (Usborne First Reading) retold by Russell Punter

Toad Makes a Road by Phil Roxbee Cox

Trucktown Series by various authors

Rhyming Books

A Pocketful of Posies by Salley Mavor

Bear Snores On by Karma Wilson

Brown Bear, Brown Bear, What Do You See? By Bill Martin Jr.

Dinosaur Roar! by Paul Stickland

Five Little Monkeys Wash the Car by Eileen Christelow

Goodnight Moon by Margaret Wise Brown

Jamberry by Bruce Degen

King Hugo's Huge Ego by Chris Van Dusen

Llama Llama Red Pajama by Anna Dewdney

How Do Dinosaurs? Series by Jane Yolen

Nursery Rhymes Color and Activity Book by Roger Priddy

Rhyming Dust Bunnies by Jan Thomas

Silly Sally by Audrey Wood

The Butt Book by Artie Bennett

The Foot Book by Dr. Seuss

The Pout-Pout Fish by Deborah Diesen

There Was an Odd Princess Who Swallowed a Pea by Jennifer Ward

Truckery Rhymes by Jon Scieszka

We're Going on a Bear Hunt by Michael Rosen

Scary Books

100 Scariest Things on the Planet by Anna Claybourne

Adventures of the Bailey School Kids Series by Debbie Dadey

Coraline by Neil Gaiman

Crooked Hills by Cullen Bunn

Deadtime Series by Annette Cascone and Gina Cascone

Deep and Dark and Dangerous: A Ghost Story by Mary Downing Hahn

Ghosthunters Series by Cornelia Funke

Goosebumps Series by R. L. Stine

Half Minute Horrors edited by Susan Rich

Monster Moon Series by BBH McChiller

Never Kick a Ghost by Judy Sierra

Nightmare Academy Series by Dean Lorey

Nightmare Hour: Time for Terror by R. L. Stein

Scary School Series by Derek the Ghost and Scott M. Fischer

Scary Stories Treasury by Alvin Schwartz

Short and Shivery Series by Robert D. San Souci

Skary Children by Katy Towell

Skeleton Man Series by Joseph Bruchac

Splurch Academy for Disruptive Boys Series by Julie Gardner Berry

A Tale of Dark and Grimm by Adam Gidwitz

The Books of Elsewhere Series by Jacqueline West

The Boy of a Thousand Faces by Brian Selznick

The Red Ghost by Marion Dane Bauer

The Scary States of America by Michael Teitelbaum

The Stoker Legacy Series by A. G. Kent

Sporty Books

A Running Back Can't Always Rush by Nate LeBoutillier

Backyard Sports Series by Michael Teitelbaum

Ballet Sisters Series by Jan Ormerod

Ballpark Mysteries Series by David A. Kelly

Baseball Card Adventure Series by Dan Gutman

Big Book of Why Sports Edition by Sports Illustrated Kids

Catcher with a Glass Arm by Matt Christopher

Cork and Fuzz: Good Sports by Dori Chaconas

Goof-Off Goalie by Betty Hicks

Guinness World Records Super Sports by Shirley Pearson

Guys Read: The Sports Pages edited by Jon Scieszka

How Angel Peterson Got His Name by Gary Paulsen

McKenna, Ready to Fly (American Girl Series) by Mary Cassanova

Mudville by Kurtis Scaletta

Soccer Sam by Jean Marzollo

Sports Illustrated Kids Graphic Novel Series by Various Authors

Sports Illustrated Kids Victory School Superstars Series by Various Authors

The Great Quarterback Switch by Matt Christopher

The Sports Fairies Series by Daisy Meadows

Xtreme Sports by Paul E. Nunn

iPad Books

A Charlie Brown Christmas

Anamalia

Andrew Answers

Are You My Friend?

Bartelby's Book of Buttons Vol. 1

Bert and Ernie's Great Adventures What's Cooking?

Bizzy Bear Builds a House

Blue Hat Green Hat

Bob Books #1

Boom Bah!

Cinderella A 3-D Fairy Tale

It's Almost Time

Legend of Spookley the Square Pumpkin

Little Critter All By Myself

Little Mermaid

Millie Was Here

Mr. Brown Can Moo, How About You?

Nancy Drew

Oh, the Thinks You Can Think

Pat the Bunny

Penguin's Family The Story of a Humboldt Penguin

Polar Bear Horizon

Sir Charlie Stinky Socks and the Really Big Adventure

Tacky Goes to Camp

The Berenstain Bears' Bedtime Battle

The Fantastic Flying Books of Mr. Morris Lessmore

The Going to Bed Book

The Monster At the End of this Book

The Three Little Pigs 3D

There's a Wocket in My Pocket

This Too Shall Pass

Triceratops Gets Lost

Van Gogh and the Sunflowers

Weird But True

What Does the President Look Like?

Where do Balloons Go?

Additional Resources and Printables

Computer Programs

ABCya!
Click-N-Kids
Jumpstart
PBS Kids PLAY
Raz-Kids
Reading Eggs
Rusty and Rosy Reading
Story Time for Me

Computer e-book Library

International Children's Digital Library (ICDL)

Book Love

About Melissa Taylor

A mother of two girls and an award-winning educator, Melissa Taylor holds a Master's Degree in Global Education, with expertise in early childhood and elementary education and a focus on literacy and play. She has taught all subjects for the elementary grades and preschool.

Bilingual in English and Spanish, Taylor has taught English as a Second Language, taught Spanish-speaking children in inner-city Denver Public Schools and in the federal migrant program, and served as a literacy trainer in underperforming schools for the Public Education & Business Coalition (PEBC). She was a four-time consecutive winner of Outstanding Teacher in Douglas County.

Melissa writes about education, learning, children's literature, technology, and advocacy for publications online and in print, including *Parenting.com, USA Today Health, The Writer, Scholastic Parent and Child, Working Mother.com, Babble.com, Colorado Parent Magazine, Denver Magazine.* In 2010, she won the coveted Colorado delegate spot for Parenting Magazine's Education and Learning Mom Congress. In January 2012, *Entrepreneur* magazine featured Taylor as the "'Trep of the Month."

Melissa created and writes the highly popular and award-winning learning blog Imagination Soup. Imagination Soup is a PBS Kids VIP Blog and was selected as the Scholastic Parent and Child Magazine Best Reading & Book Blog for 2010, as well as for the Circle of Moms Top 25 Teacher Mom Blogs and Top 25 Tech Moms.

Melissa served as a panelist for the Cybils 2011 Book Apps and the 2010 Early Readers & Early Chapter Books. She is a member of the American Society of Journalists and Authors (ASJA), Education Writers Association and the Denver Woman's Press Club.

For more information about Melissa, please visit her website.

Appendix

Links to Referenced Articles and Recommended Products

Chapter Two

8 Reasons Why Kids Should Read Comics http://bit.ly/Rvikf0

Headlamp http://bit.ly/OZh1H8

Pointer http://bit.ly/QDJAZ4

Monster Finger Pointer http://bit.ly/WGbtEO

Student Pointers Set of 8 http://bit.ly/XP5iwf

Harry Potter Wand and Bookmark Set http://bit.ly/XP5iwf

Magnetic I-Clips http://bit.ly/POuiE2

Wizards and Dragons http://bit.ly/RisQqp

Chapter Three

Colored Overlays http://bit.ly/TvXYqL

Reading Trackers http://bit.ly/RSBD1n

Reading Guide Strips http://bit.ly/RitB2E

FitBall Seating Disc http://bit.ly/RSBRFK

Chapter Four

Magnetic Letters http://bit.ly/WGdq43

Pointer http://bit.ly/SmQMIR

Reader Strips http://bit.ly/SmQMIR

See-Through Bookmarks http://bit.ly/VmcexE

Star Alphabet Posters http://bit.ly/X8ONvz

Chapter Five

E-book Reading Strategies http://bit.ly/TdogMm

White Elephant Gift Exchange Rules http://bit.ly/TEa8HZ

School Library Journal's Top 100 Picture Books http://bit.ly/XPbXXp

My Magical Cushion http://bit.ly/T8Gz0E

Chew Stixx http://bit.ly/UxoMXh

Modern Ball Chair http://bit.ly/TdpFCH

Headlamp http://bit.ly/Po6rec

IPod Touch http://bit.ly/RTzfXD

Headphones http://bit.ly/Po6ved

Indoor Swing http://amzn.to/RTzmTi

Mind Putty http://bit.ly/VmekgZ

Fold-and-Go Trampoline http://bit.ly/XPeNeI

Chapter Six

Alphabetical Adventure http://bbc.in/XPfa9o

Alphabet Wack-a-Mole http://bit.ly/TdqlYB

The ABC's Zoo Learning Game http://bit.ly/Tw3oln

ABC Cookies Goodie Games http://bit.ly/RTCFtI

ABC Punch Out Blocks http://bit.ly/VmhP78

Alphabet Blocks http://bit.ly/POB1h4

Foam http://bit.ly/QSsFA4

Magnetic http://bit.ly/RfcnVo

Foam and Magnetic http://bit.ly/RfcnVo

Alphabet Music http://bit.ly/POBdgg

Alphabet Pebbles http://bit.ly/TQBZ8t

Alphabet Puzzle http://bit.ly/Rizygb

Alphabet Soup Sorters http://bit.ly/Sn6G5Y

Alphabet Stamps http://bit.ly/RvIBK2

Aquadoodle http://bit.ly/S0ByvD

Fridge Phonics http://bit.ly/WGnRo8

Lacing Alphabet http://bit.ly/TQDS4O

Letter Matching Game http://bit.ly/OZvsLm

Magnadoodle http://bit.ly/WGnRo8

POP for Letters Game Alphabet Awareness - http://bit.ly/UxCrhd

Purpllinker http://bit.ly/T8NyGX

Smart Snacks ABC Lacing Sweets http://bit.ly/TdvC2f

Wikki-Stix Alphabet Cards http://bit.ly/RTG8br

Wipe Clean Letters http://bit.ly/RfdrIR

Chapter Seven

Super Grover's The Nick of Rhyme http://to.pbs.org/TQGL5N

Sesame Street: Rhyming Day http://bit.ly/S0EIPW

Rhyming Games http://to.pbs.org/WGqt5F

Six Games for Reading http://bit.ly/TwbVVw

What's in the Work Box? http://bit.ly/UxEHFa

Eboo Rhyming Word Puzzle Pairs http://bit.ly/TdwPXq

Fingerplays and Rhymes in a Jar http://bit.ly/TwcZIR

My Book of Rhyming Words http://bit.ly/VmmxSB

Nir! Games: Rhyming War! http://bit.ly/RvRkMn

Picture Rhymes Concentration http://bit.ly/WGrN8B

Really Good Rhyming Kit http://bit.ly/RvRkMn

Rhyming Bingo http://bit.ly/Sg9mE7

Rhyming Marks the Spot Floor Game http://bit.ly/RSTJQE

Rhyming Puzzle Cards http://bit.ly/S0GII3

Rhyming Words Workbook http://bit.ly/UxGGt2

The Complete Book and CD Set of Rhymes, Songs, Poems, Fingerplays, and Chants http://bit.ly/TEiq2O

Word Building Game Chunks http://bit.ly/TEiq2O

Zingo Bingo with a Zing http://bit.ly/RffexK

Chapter Eight

Link 26 http://bit.ly/TEjYd0

Montessori Phonetic Object Box http://etsy.me/TEk0Sa

Montessori Phonetic Reading Blocks http://etsy.me/RfgQaz

Phonics iPad Apps http://bit.ly/T8R7x0

POP for Word Families http://bit.ly/RiEWj6

Reading Rods http://bit.ly/Snmd5N

Sandpaper Letters http://bit.ly/T8Rdoj

Snatch-It http://bit.ly/RiF3eE

Spell It http://bit.ly/TdA8Om

Toobaloo http://bit.ly/XPBiAd

Word Families Slide and Learn http://bit.ly/Tdy8pe

Chapter Nine

Tools for Educators http://www.toolsforeducators.com/bingo

Print Bingo http://www.print-bingo.com

Alphabet Stamps http://bit.ly/RvIBK2

Bananagrams http://bit.ly/RiFxRV

Storymaker Magnetic Poetry Kit http://bit.ly/Rw16y3

Magnetic Sight Words http://bit.ly/XPCMug

POP for Sight Words Game http://bit.ly/RfhB3F

Sight Words Books http://bit.ly/RSYNVj

Sight Word Bingo http://bit.ly/QE06YY

Sight Word Flash Cards http://book-love.net
Sight Word Plastic Tiles http://bit.ly/UxOSJI
Sight Word String Up Set http://bit.ly/S0OeTa
uKloo Treasure Hunt http://ukloo.com
What's Gnu? http://bit.ly/TQPp45
Zingo! Bingo with a Zing http://bit.ly/RiG7iH

Chapter Ten

Between the Lions http://to.pbs.org/QE0VkA
Easi-Speak USB Recorder http://bit.ly/T8SBar
Fluency Timer http://bit.ly/Sgejg8
Nir! Now I'm Reading Plays http://bit.ly/Rw4iJX
Silly Sentences http://bit.ly/Rw4rwQ
Reading Plus http://readingplus.com
Raz-Kids http://raz-kids.com
Hidden Hints http://bit.ly/TQQvNl
Capture the Flag http://bit.ly/TQQOb6
Book Mission Kit http://bit.ly/PojUmu

Notes

1. *reading aloud* C.J. Lonigan, C. J., C. Schatschneider, & L. Westberg, (2008). Identification of children's skills and abilities linked to later outcomes in reading, writing, and spelling. In National Early Literacy Panel, Developing early literacy: Report of the National Early Literacy Panel (pp. 55-106). Washington DC: National Institute for Literacy. Available at http://www.nil.gov/earlycholdhood/NELP/NELPreport.html.

2. Jane Healy, Different Learners (New York: Simon & Schuster, 2010).

3. *emotions* David Sousa, How the Brain Learns (Thousand Oaks, Corwin Press, 2006), 44.

4. *sleep* David Sousa, How the Brain Learns (Thousand Oaks, Corwin Press, 2006), 102.

5. *Sensory Processing Disorder* Lucy Jane Miller, Ph.D., OTR, Sensational Kids: Hope and Help for Children wit Sensory Processing Disorder, (New York, Perigree, 2006,) 5.

6. *good reader strategies* Ellen Keene and Susan Zimmerman. Mosaic of Thought. (Portsmouth, Heinemann, 1997)

CPSIA information can be obtained at www.ICGtesting.com
Printed in the USA
LVOW01s1944260514

387277LV00008B/41/P